WHAT IS AN
AMPHIBIAN?

Robert Snedden

Photographs by Oxford Scientific Films

Illustrated by Adrian Lascom

Sierra Club Books for Children
San Francisco

The Sierra Club, founded in 1892 by John Muir, has devoted itself to the study and protection of the earth's scenic and ecological resources — mountains, wetlands, woodlands, wild shores and rivers, deserts and plains. The publishing program of the Sierra Club offers books to the public as a nonprofit educational service in the hope that they may enlarge the public's understanding of the Club's basic concerns. The Sierra Club has some sixty chapters in the United States and in Canada. For information about how you may participate in its programs to preserve wilderness and the quality of life, please address inquiries to Sierra Club, 730 Polk Street, San Francisco, CA 94109.

First U.S. Edition 1994

First published in Great Britain in 1993 by Belitha Press Limited, 31 Newington Green, London N16 9PU

Library of Congress Cataloging-in-Publication Data

Snedden, Robert.
      What is an amphibian?/Robert Snedden; photographs by Oxford Scientific Films; illustrated by Adrian Lascom.
          p.   cm.
      "First published in Great Britain in 1993 by Belitha Press Limited"—T.p. verso.
      Includes index.
      Summary: Defines amphibians and describes their lives, including their maturation, mating, sense perception, and feeding.
      ISBN 0-87156-469-6
      1. Amphibians—Juvenile literature.
[1. Amphibians.] I. Lascom, Adrian, ill. II. Oxford Scientific Films. III. Title.
QL644.2.S69 1994
597.6—dc20   93—11619

Printed in Hong Kong for Imago
10 9 8 7 6 5 4 3 2 1

Editor: Rachel Cooke
Series designer: Frances McKay
Designer: Vivienne Gordon
Consultant: Dr. Jim Flegg
Educational consultant: Brenda Hart

The publisher wishes to thank the following for permission to reproduce copyrighted material:

Oxford Scientific Films and individual copyright holders on the following pages: Kathie Atkinson, 7 top; G.I. Bernard, 8 bottom, 23, 24; Mike Birkhead, 27 right; Martyn Chillmaid, 5 bottom; Dr. J. A. L. Cooke, 16 top, 19 bottom; Jack Dermid, 3, 21, left; Michael Fogden, 9 both, 13, 18, 25 top, 28–29; Paul Franklin, 4 right, 7 bottom left; Jim Frazier/Mantis Wildlife Films, 27 left; Breck P. Kent/Animals Animals, 8 top, 25 bottom; R. K. La Val/Animals Animals, 4 left; Michael Leach, 11 bottom, 20 top; Zig Leszczynski/Animals Animals, cover, 1, 6, 7 center right, 11 top, 19 top, 20 bottom, 21 right, 22; Mike Linley, 5 top, 10, 12; Stan Osolinski, 26; Avril Ramage, 17; Alastair Shay, 16 bottom.

Front cover picture: These red-eyed leaf frogs live in the rain forests of Central America.

Title page picture: The Colorado River toad is found in North America.

Contents page picture: North America is also home to the colorful cave salamander.

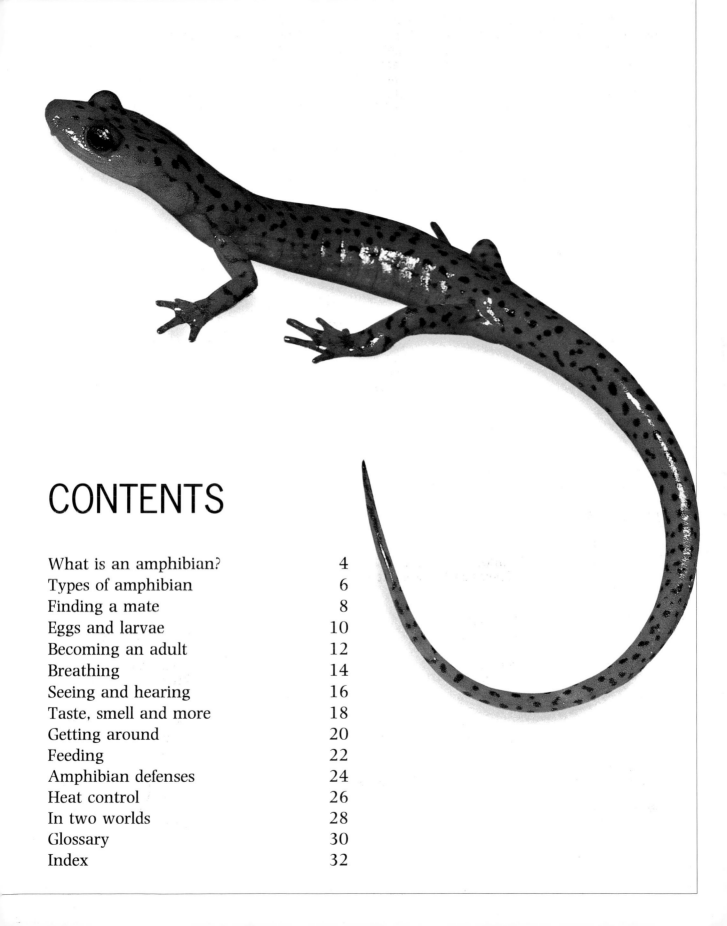

CONTENTS

WHAT IS AN AMPHIBIAN?

What do you think an amphibian is? It is a word you may have come across if you have studied frogs, which are one of the commonest types of amphibian. Perhaps you have noticed that frogs seem to spend much of their time near water. One of the things that makes amphibians different from other animals is the importance of water to them. This book will show you the ways in which amphibians are adapted for life on land and in water.

If you have ever watched the way in which legless swimming tadpoles turn into swimming and jumping frogs, then you have seen one of the most fasci-

▼ Crested newts, like this one, are common throughout northern Europe.

▲ This emerald glass frog from Central America has very thin skin. If you look carefully you can see inside its body.

nating things about amphibians — the way they change from one form into another. You'll find out more about this change later in the book.

Amphibians include such animals as frogs, toads, newts and salamanders. They come in a variety of sizes, shapes and colors. Some amphibians have tails and some don't. Almost all **adult** amphibians have four legs. There are some, however, that have no legs and look like grey worms more than three feet long. Some are very brightly colored. But all amphibians have certain features in common. This book will show you what those special features are.

▼ A fire salamander from Germany. Newts and salamanders are similar types of amphibian.

▲ A natterjack toad. Toads are very similar to frogs but often have thicker skins.

5

TYPES OF AMPHIBIAN

There are three basic types of amphibian. There are amphibians that have legs and tails, amphibians that have legs but no tails, and amphibians that have tails but no legs.

The amphibians with legs and tails are the salamanders and newts. Most are just a few inches long, but the biggest can be more than five feet. Salamanders usually have four legs, a short body and a tail. Most are brightly colored. Some salamanders live their entire lives in water; others live on the land and only spend the first part of their lives in water. There are also salamanders that live in trees and some that burrow in the ground.

The tailless amphibians are the frogs and toads. The tiniest frog is only a half-inch long when fully grown; the largest can be more than three feet. Frogs and toads usually have long hind legs for jumping, a short body and a big head. Frogs can be found on land and in water. Toads tend to live mostly on land. Frogs and toads can be found almost anywhere there is a supply of fresh water. There are a huge variety of frogs and toads. Many of them are very brightly colored.

▼ Adult salamanders have four legs and a tail. This is a northern red salamander.

▲ Cane toads are the largest type of toad. Like other amphibians, they are active hunters. This cane toad is eating a pygmy possum.

▶ Caecilians are unusual amphibians that don't have legs. Their segmented skin makes them look like earthworms.

A tiny tree frog on a toadstool.

The limbless amphibians, those without legs, are called caecilians. They have a long body and a short tail. Their skin is divided into segments, making them look a bit like earthworms. They usually burrow in the ground in damp soil and have a thick skull to help force their way through the ground, though one type lives in streams. Caecilians range in size from about six inches to more than four feet in length. They are found only in hot, wet, tropical climates.

FINDING A MATE

Like most other animals, an amphibian must find a **mate** before it can have young. All adult female amphibians produce eggs. These eggs are **fertilized** by a male amphibian so that they will produce new young amphibians.

Many amphibians, especially frogs and toads, will return to the pond or stream where they were born in order to find a mate. Often they have to travel several miles to get there. Usually, large numbers of males arrive first. To begin with, the males are silent, but after a few days they begin to call loudly to one another. This shouting match is actually a battle for **territory**. The one that calls loudest usually wins. Later the females arrive and the males try to attract them, using a different call.

Newts don't make calls. Instead, the male newt attracts a female by dancing and waving a special scent with his tail. Nobody really knows how male and female caecilians find each other.

◀ A male American toad (on top) fertilizing a female's eggs.

▼ The male great crested newt (on the right) is trying to attract the female (on the left) by dancing.

Most female frogs and toads lay their eggs in water. Before this happens, a male frog climbs onto a female's back. As she lays her eggs, the male frog pours a milky fluid over them to fertilize them. Male newts and salamanders lay tiny jelly-like packages called **sperm-atophores**. The females then take these into a special opening in their bodies called a **cloaca**. Inside the female's body the jelly dissolves and fertilizes the eggs before they are laid. Male caecilians are able to fertilize a female's eggs directly inside her body.

Some types of newts, salamanders and caecilians don't lay their eggs. Instead, they remain inside the female's body, where they develop into young animals. The next two pages provide a closer look at the way amphibians' eggs develop.

▲ A male frog sometimes attracts a mate by calling. It does this by puffing up the vocal sac in its throat.

Sometimes male frogs fight each other to see which one gets the female. The fighting frogs here are strawberry arrow-poison frogs.

EGGS AND LARVAE

The eggs of an amphibian are not like those of a bird. Birds' eggs have a hard shell to protect them, but amphibians' eggs have only a coating of jelly and must be protected from drying out. This is one reason why amphibians must find somewhere wet to lay their eggs.

Some types of amphibian take great care of their eggs. Some female salamanders guard them by curling their bodies around them. Some frogs and toads carry their eggs around with them. For example, male midwife toads carry their eggs wrapped around their waists. The male is always careful to find places where the eggs won't dry out. When the eggs are about to hatch, he returns to a pond. There he puts his back legs in the water and the eggs hatch out. One type of male frog keeps the eggs safe inside the throat pouch he usually uses to make his calls. When the eggs hatch, the young emerge from his mouth. Many types of amphibian lay thousands of eggs and then simply abandon them. A lot of the eggs are eaten by other animals, such as fish.

The young that hatch from the eggs of amphibians are called **larvae**. The larvae of salamanders and newts look a bit like adults without legs or like very small fish. They have feathery **gills** on their bodies that let them breathe underwater. Most eat small water animals, such as water fleas, and some eat algae and other tiny plants.

◀ Some amphibians take good care of their eggs. This male midwife toad will carry his until they are ready to hatch.

◄ This marbled sala-
mander guards its
eggs by wrapping its
body around them
until they hatch.

The larvae of frogs and toads are usually called tadpoles. Tadpoles have tails and no legs and look nothing like the adults. Tadpoles also have gills. At first, their gills are on the outside of their bodies. Later they grow new gills inside and the outside ones disappear. A tadpole doesn't have a mouth when it hatches. It is still attached to the yolk from its egg, and this supplies it with food until its mouth appears. Then the tadpole will eat plants and after a while other small animals.

Did you know?

Robber frogs are unusual as they lay their eggs on land and don't go through a tadpole stage. Instead, tiny, fully developed frogs hatch from the eggs. Each young frog has a little spine on its upper jaw to help it slice its way out of the egg.

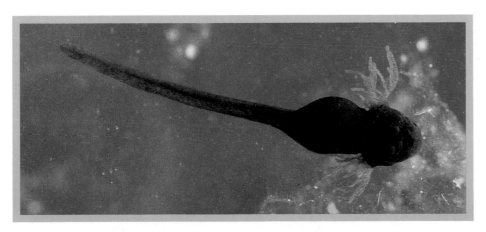

◄ A young tadpole
showing the feathery
gills it uses for
breathing underwater.
When it is older it will
have gills inside its
body.

BECOMING AN ADULT

Amphibians are not the only animals whose young look different from the adults. Insects also have larvae that must change to become adults. Insect larvae usually go through a resting stage to change, but amphibian larvae change into adults while they are active.

The change from a larva into an adult is called **metamorphosis**. One of the first signs that a frog tadpole is changing is when it begins to make trips to the surface of the water to take in gulps of air. This is because its **lungs** are starting to develop. It will use these to breathe air as an adult. An adult amphibian has to breathe air to get all the **oxygen** it needs. Only the larvae have the gills that are needed for underwater breathing.

Next the tadpole's back legs appear and its tail begins to disappear back into its body. The tail helps provide the

▲ Unusually for amphibians, alpine salamanders don't lay eggs but give birth to fully developed young.

▼ Most frogs and toads develop in the same way. They hatch from eggs as swimming tadpoles with a tail and no legs. First their back legs grow. Then the tail begins to shrink and their front legs appear. They grow lungs on the inside and their gills disappear. Finally they are ready to climb out onto land.

back legs develop

young tadpole

frog eggs

fully grown tadpole

front legs develop

◀ Salamanders known as axolotls never really grow up. Even when fully grown, they still have gills.

changing tadpole with a supply of food. The front legs appear, the eyes grow bigger and the shape of the tadpole changes to look more like an adult frog or toad. Finally the tiny animal leaves the water and can move around on land.

Newts and salamanders change in a similar way, but their front legs appear first and the larvae keep their gills on the outside of their bodies until their lungs develop. Caecilians never grow legs at all. The only difference between the larvae and the adults is that the larvae have gills.

fully grown frog

young frog
(tail disappearing)

BREATHING

All animals need **oxygen** to stay alive. Oxygen lets them use the energy in the food they eat. Animals get oxygen by breathing. Some animals breathe in oxygen from the air; others, such as fish, get it from water. Amphibians can do both. Oxygen passes into the animal's blood through any very thin, moist surface with **blood vessels** beneath it. The oxygen is then carried around the animal's body in the blood to where it is needed.

Most adult amphibians breathe using simple lungs. These are like very thin bags inside their bodies. They are lined with tiny blood vessels. The amphibians take air into their lungs and the oxygen passes into the blood vessels.

An amphibian does not breathe only with its lungs. It can also breathe through its skin. The skin of an amphibian is different from that of other animals. It is very thin and feels smooth and moist to the touch. It is covered in a slimy substance called **mucus**. There

blood vessel

poison gland (see page 25)

blood vessel

mucus gland

▼ An adult frog's lungs are lined with blood vessels. These extract the oxygen from the air it breathes in. The oxygen then moves through the body in the blood, which is pumped around by the frog's heart. Glands in the frog's skin produce the mucus that keeps its skin moist and also enables it to breathe through its skin.

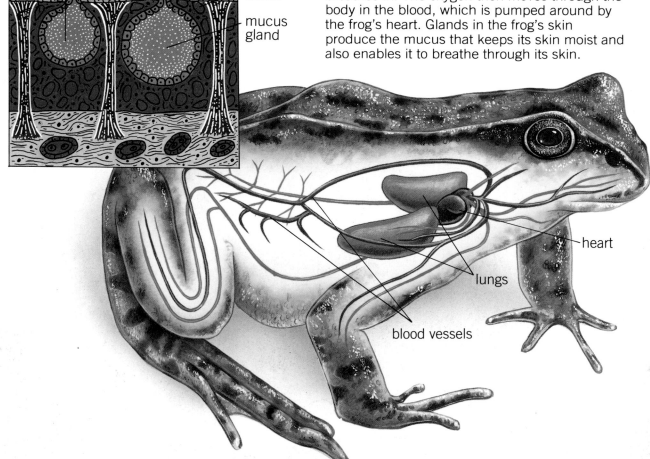

heart

lungs

blood vessels

are also a great many blood vessels just under the surface of the skin. Oxygen dissolves in the mucus coat and from there it passes into the blood vessels under the skin. An amphibian can get oxygen through its skin from water as well as air.

Amphibians can also breathe through the moist lining of their mouths. Air is drawn into the mouth through the nostrils. The inside of the mouth is lined with a great many blood vessels. As you might guess, the same thing happens in the mouth as on the skin and in the

lungs. Oxygen passes from the air into the blood. Some salamanders don't have any lungs and breathe only through the skin and mouth.

Most young amphibian larvae spend their time underwater before they turn into adults. They do not have lungs at first. Instead, they breathe through feathery gills. The gills have a large number of tiny blood vessels that can absorb oxygen from the water. The gills may be on the outside or the inside of the body depending on the age of the larva and the type of amphibian it is.

▼ The feathery gills are just behind the head of this almost-grown newt. They are filled with tiny blood vessels. Oxygen from the water moves into these blood vessels.

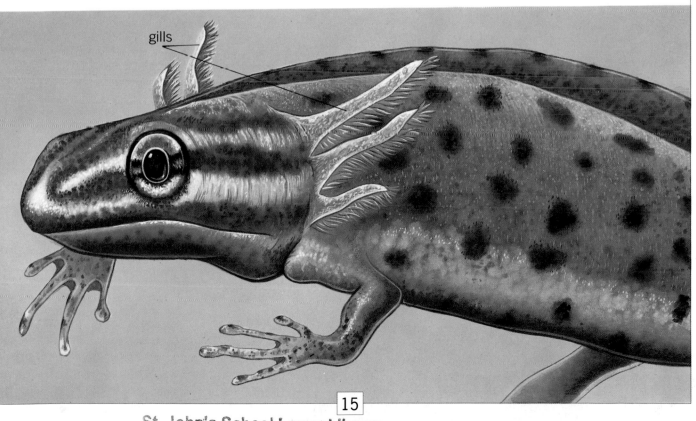

gills

SEEING AND HEARING

Sight is a very important sense for almost all amphibians. Salamanders and frogs have the best eyesight. Frogs' eyes are particularly good at picking out moving objects, especially anything that comes into view traveling from right to left or left to right. This gives them an excellent chance of spotting any insects going by. A frog won't touch an insect that isn't moving. Most amphibians can probably see in color. Many of them are brightly colored, particularly during the **mating season**.

Caecilians spend most of their time burrowing in the ground and are prac-tically blind. Their eyes are covered by skin and sometimes bone.

Frogs and toads cannot see very well underwater. Their large eyes often stick up above the water like the periscope of a submarine while the rest of the animal stays submerged. This helps to keep the animal hidden, perhaps from a bird that might want to eat it. Having

▲ Caecilians do not have good eyesight.

If you look carefully at this frog, you can see one of its eardrums. It is the little circle just behind its eye.

eyes on the top of the head is also useful for tree frogs. They can see all around them and keep watch for possible danger or food.

All amphibians can hear. Frogs and toads have **eardrums** that are like tightly stretched pieces of skin just behind their eyes. The eardrums can pick up sound vibrations in air and in water. Frogs and toads have the best hearing of all amphibians. They have many different calls to **communicate** with one another. They may have one call to attract a mate, a call to warn off rivals, a call to warn other frogs of danger, and even a call they use when it is raining. It is important that a frog knows what other frogs are saying.

▼ The bulging eyes of a frog enable it to keep a lookout while most of its body stays hidden under the water.

Did you know?

Sometimes when a male toad is looking for a mate he may grab another male by mistake. If this happens, the male that is grabbed makes a special call that says, "Let me go!" to the other toad.

TASTE, SMELL AND MORE

An animal's sense of taste can tell it if something is good to eat or drink. An amphibian tastes using its tongue, which has **taste buds**, just like your tongue does. These taste buds send signals to the brain, which determines if it is a good or bad taste. Many types of insect protect themselves from being eaten by having a foul taste. If a toad or other amphibian catches an insect that tastes bad it will quickly spit it out.

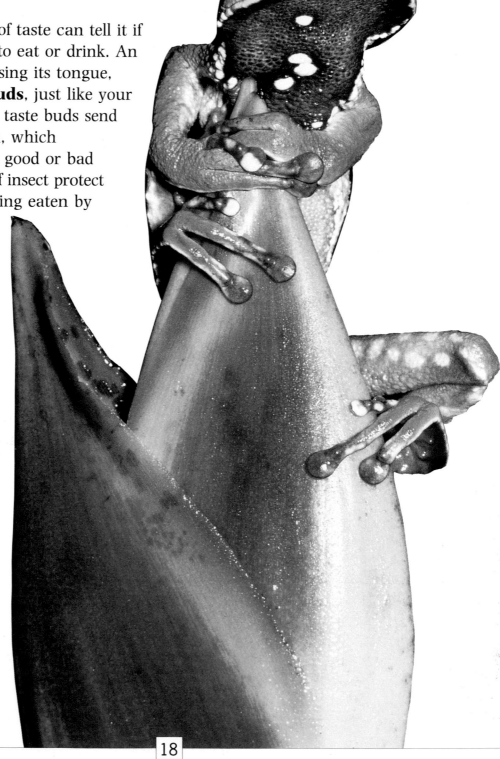

▶ Sitting on top of a plant, this leaf frog can use its senses of sight and smell to find out what is going on around it.

Smells travel through the air as very tiny particles. Amphibians have a thin, moist lining inside their nostrils. The tiny particles in the air dissolve in this moist lining when they are breathed in through the nose. Special detectors in the lining send signals to the part of the amphibian's brain that deals with smells. The brain then tries to determine from the signals what the smell is. Your nose works in much the same way. Newts often find their food by smelling it. They can become very excited when they find something they can eat and may attack other newts that come too near. Blind caecilians rely heavily on their sense of smell to find out what is around them.

The sense of touch can give an animal a lot of information about its surroundings. Amphibians can detect

▲ A clawed toad has a line of special detectors in its skin called the lateral line, which can pick up tiny movements in the water.

vibrations traveling through water or through the ground. These vibrations might be made by a possible mate or a meal nearby. Touch is an important sense for burrowing amphibians such as caecilians and some toads. A few amphibians have a line of detectors in their skin that are particularly good at picking up vibrations traveling through water. This line of detectors is called a **lateral line**. It lets the amphibian know when something is moving near it in the water. Fish have lateral lines as well.

▼ This toad is about to eat an insect. Taste buds on its tongue will tell it if the insect is good to eat. If it is not, the toad will spit it out very quickly.

Did you know?

A male smooth newt tries hard to attract a female. He shows off his brilliant color and waves his tail to send his smell to her through the water, which also makes a current of water that she can feel at the same time. It is difficult for the female to ignore the male since she can see, smell and feel him.

GETTING AROUND

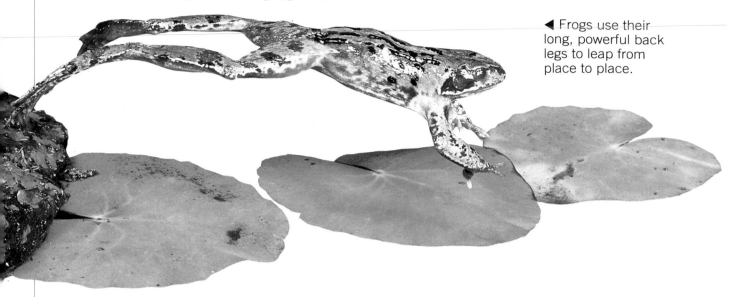

◄ Frogs use their long, powerful back legs to leap from place to place.

Amphibians get from place to place in a variety of ways. The legless caecilians burrow in soft ground. They use their heads like shovels and force their bodies into the ground with their strong muscles, bending from side to side a little like swimming fish.

▲ The spadefoot toad's back foot has webbing between its toes. It also has a special hard spur that it uses for burrowing.

Most frogs and toads have back legs that are much longer than their front legs. A frog's back legs are often very powerful and are usually used for jumping. The frog uses its strong thigh muscles to straighten its back legs, pushing them hard against the ground to propel itself through the air. The front legs are also used when it is walking along the ground. Toads don't jump like frogs. They hop or walk along the ground. Almost all frogs and toads swim in the same way – pushing their back legs against the water to thrust themselves forward and using their front legs to steer with. **Webbing** between the toes of the back feet helps the amphibian push more effectively – just like a human diver's flippers.

Some types of frog that live in trees are able to glide through the air for short distances. They do this by stretching out the thin webbing between their long toes. The webbing acts like little glider wings and keeps the frog in the air longer by making it fall more slowly.

Newts and salamanders that spend most of their time on the ground stand with their feet far apart. As they walk, they bend their bodies from side to side so as to make each step as long as possible. Newts that live in water use their legs very little. They swim by moving their whole bodies in an S shape, a bit like a swimming fish or a burrowing caecilian.

Amphibian larvae swim by lashing their tails from side to side.

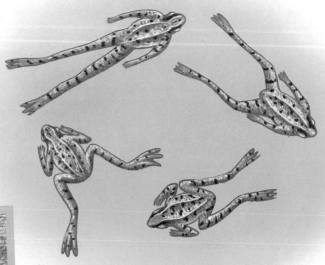

▲ A frog swims in a similar way to a human doing the breaststroke. Its webbed feet act like a human diver's flippers, pushing it swiftly through the water.

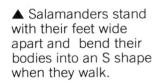

▲ Salamanders stand with their feet wide apart and bend their bodies into an S shape when they walk.

▶ The thin webbing between the toes of this gliding frog act like tiny glider wings when it jumps from branch to branch.

FEEDING

Many amphibians will eat whatever food they can find that is small enough to be eaten. Most amphibians are meat eaters. Larger types of frogs and toads will eat small mammals, birds, fish and reptiles. Others will eat insects, snails or the larvae of other amphibians. Most of the salamanders and newts feed on insects, worms, slugs and similar animals. Young amphibians from the same cluster of eggs will even eat each other if there is nothing else to eat.

Amphibians' teeth are in two parts – each tooth has an upper **crown** and a thin section that attaches it to the jaw. The teeth are used for gripping food and not for cutting or chewing. All of an amphibian's teeth are the same size and shape. However, a few amphibians have no teeth at all.

Many frogs and toads have a long tongue that they use to catch their

This tree frog is about to swallow a cricket that it has caught on its sticky tongue.

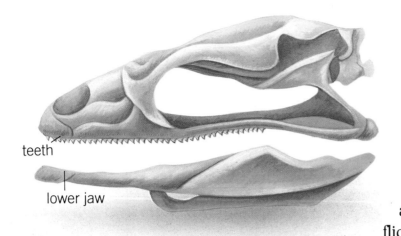

◄ You can see that the row of tiny teeth in this frog's skull are all the same. All amphibians with teeth have teeth like these.

teeth

lower jaw

prey. On the end of the tongue are special **glands** that produce a sticky substance. The frog or toad can flick its tongue out and in again in a fraction of a second, trapping moving insects on the sticky tip. The tongue is attached near the front of the mouth, not at the back, like yours. This means that it can reach farther. Some salamanders have tongues that are as long as their bodies and can flick them out to catch their food. Frogs that feed in the water catch their prey by gulping it into their mouths. When a frog or toad swallows, its eyes are withdrawn into its head, helping to push the food down its throat.

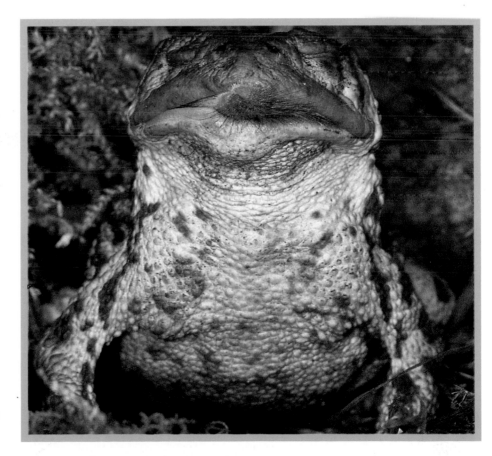

► As this toad swallows a harvest mouse its eyes withdraw into its head, helping to push the meal down its throat.

AMPHIBIAN DEFENSES

Amphibians are eaten by a great many other animals. Mammals, birds and reptiles will eat them if they can, so amphibians have a number of defenses against attack.

One of the best ways to avoid being attacked is not to be seen. Many amphibians will stay very still and hide if danger threatens. Some also have colors that help to **camouflage** them by blending into their surroundings. Caecilians can stay well hidden by burrowing under the ground.

▶ This tree frog would be difficult to see from a distance because it is the same color as the leaves it is hiding in.

Some amphibians don't try to hide themselves at all. In fact, they are very brightly colored and seem almost to attract attention to themselves. Their colors are actually a warning. These amphibians have glands in their skin that produce poison (see page 14). Other animals soon learn that these amphibians are not good to eat. Some frogs are so poisonous that they will kill any animal that eats them. A few amphibians that aren't poisonous have copied the colors of the poisonous ones so that they don't get eaten either.

Many frogs and toads try to discourage attackers by making themselves look bigger. They blow themselves up with air and sometimes raise themselves off the ground at the same time. As well as making them look more impressive, this also makes them harder to swallow.

▲ Arrow-poison frogs are so poisonous that people use the poison on their arrow tips. That's how the frog got its name.

Some salamanders try to escape from attackers by giving up their tails. When the animal is attacked, its tail breaks off. As the attacker's attention is focused on the twitching tail, the salamander makes its escape. It eventually grows a new tail.

▶ The slimy salamander defends itself by producing a sticky substance that clogs up the nose of any animal that tries to eat it.

HEAT CONTROL

Amphibians can become very slow moving when they are cold. To keep active, it helps to stay warm. Unlike birds and mammals, which can make their own warmth from inside their bodies, amphibians have to warm themselves from the outside when they are cold. They may do this by sitting in the sun, for example. Once they are warm enough they will return to the shade so that they don't get too hot.

▶ This American toad has found a warm place to sit — on the back of a turtle.

An amphibian's moist skin can cause problems for it when it is trying to keep warm. The liquid water in the mucus on the amphibian's skin turns to water vapor. When this happens it uses up a lot of heat energy and cools the amphibian down. It also means that the amphibian can lose a lot of water and might be in danger of drying out altogether. This is one reason why many amphibians live in damp places. However, some frogs that live in dry places can spend six months hiding more than three feet beneath the ground until the rain comes again. Their skin forms a thin shell to help prevent the frog from drying out.

▼ This Australian burrowing frog will stay underground until the rain comes again. Its skin has formed a waterproof shell to stop the frog from drying out.

In some places amphibians are unable to get warm enough to stay active during the cold winter months. In these conditions an amphibian will find someplace, such as the muddy bottom of a pond, where it can avoid the lowest temperatures. There it goes into a sleeplike state called **hibernation**. During hibernation its heart slows down and its body temperature drops. The amphibian may also stop breathing with its lungs and get all the oxygen it needs through its skin. A few types of frog living in North America can survive very cold conditions. More than half of the water in the frog's body can turn to ice and it will still live.

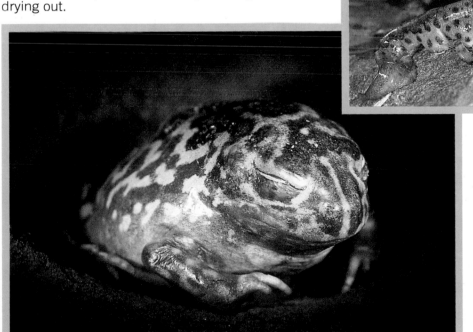

▲ This smooth newt's skin is always moist. To help keep it that way, the newt is active at night, rarely exposing itself to the heat of the day.

IN TWO WORLDS

Amphibians can be found in many parts of the world and in many brilliant colors. These golden toads are from Central America.

Amphibians are special because they spend their lives in the two worlds of water and land. As adults, amphibians are perfectly at home on land, but they usually don't stray too far from water. They must lay their eggs in a damp place to prevent them from drying out. The larvae of most amphibians hatch from eggs and swim and grow in the water, breathing through their gills. Then metamorphosis occurs, and the water-living larvae become air-breathing, land-living adults. It

is their life in water and on land that gives these animals their name. *Amphibian* means "both lives."

As often happens in nature, there are exceptions to these rules. Some toads give birth to little toadlets rather than laying eggs. Some salamanders live their entire lives in the water, never coming out onto land. What all amphibians have in common is their moist skin, which can be used for breathing. All amphibians also have gills at some time in their lives.

Millions of years ago, amphibians were the first animals to venture onto dry land. Now they can be found in many different places, from tropical rain forests to high mountain meadows. Some can be found in deserts, but only where there is some chance of rain. Amphibians are never found in the sea or in the cold regions around the poles. They are important parts of the living world – hunters of smaller animals and a source of food for others, including some fish, birds and people.

GLOSSARY

Adult: An animal that is fully grown.

Blood vessels: The network of tubes, called veins and arteries, that carry blood around inside the body.

Camouflage: Colors or patterns on something that help it blend into its surroundings, making it difficult to see. This can help an animal to hide from other animals that might want to eat it.

Cloaca: An opening in the body of many types of animal, including amphibians, birds and reptiles. Waste passes out through the cloaca. Female animals are fertilized through the cloaca and lay their eggs through it.

Communicate: To use sounds, smells or signals to tell another animal something.

Crown: The part of a tooth that can be seen inside the mouth.

Eardrum: The part of the ear in some types of animal that is made to vibrate by sound waves. These vibrations are then passed on to the part of the ear where the sound is heard.

Fertilize: To join the male sperm with the female egg so that a new animal can grow from it.

Gills: The parts of the body that many water-living animals, including young amphibians and fish, use to breathe — that is, to get oxygen from the water.

Gland: A part of the body that produces special substances needed by an animal. An amphibian's mucus glands help keep its skin moist.

Hibernation: A sleeplike state that some animals enter into as a way of surviving harsh winter conditions. During hibernation, an animal's body cools down and its heart and other body parts work more slowly.

Larva (plural: larvae): The young of an animal such as an amphibian or insect after it hatches from the egg. A larva does not look like the adult it will grow into. Frog larvae are called tadpoles.

Lateral line: Special sensors along the sides of some amphibians and most fish that can detect movement and vibration in the water.

Lungs: The parts of the body that many types of animal, including humans, use to breathe — that is, to get oxygen from the air.

Mate: One of a pair of animals — one male and the other female — that will produce young together.

Mating season: The time of year at which the males and females of a type of animal seek each other out in order to produce young.

Metamorphosis: The change from a larva into an adult that takes place in some animals, including amphibians.

Mucus: A slightly sticky fluid that is produced by special glands to protect some parts of the body. Amphibians produce mucus to protect their skin.

Oxygen: A gas found in the air and dissolved in water. Living things need oxygen to stay alive.

Prey: The name given to the animals that another animal kills and eats.

Spermatophore: A package of sperm produced by male newts and salamanders and some other animals. The female picks up the spermatophore through her cloaca in order to fertilize her eggs.

Taste buds: Tiny parts of the tongue that send signals to the brain about the way something tastes.

Territory: The area in which an animal lives and that it will defend against others. Many types of frog call out to tell others where their territory is.

Webbing: The skin between the toes of some animals, including some amphibians.

INDEX